Perennials and Roses

Cullen Garden Guide

Perennials and Roses

by Mark Cullen

Summerhill Press Ltd.
Toronto

© Mark Cullen

Published by Summerhill Press Ltd
Published by Toronto, Ontario

Cover Photography: Dieter Hessel
Editors: Tony Reynolds
Editors: Judith Drynan
Illustrations: Lynn McIlvride Evans

Canadian Cataloguing in Publication Data

Cullen, Mark, 1956-
   Perennials and roses

(Cullen Canadian garden guide)
ISBN 0-920197-25-6

1. Perennials.   2. Roses.   I. Title.
II. Series.

SB434.C84 1986   635.9'32   C86-093012-2

Distributed in Canada by:
Collier Macmillan Canada
50 Gervais Drive
Don Mills, Ontario M3C 3K4

Printed and Bound in Canada

To our second little sprout, Heather.

Contents

Letter From Mark

Almost anyone interested in having a garden, large or small, knows what annuals are. The are the colourful and fast-growing plants you buy in flats every spring — plants like petunias, marigolds and asters. These plants complete their entire growing cycle in one season and then die out in the autumn.

Less well-known to people these days are the perennial plants like bleeding hearts, peonies and delphinium. Perennial means that these plants have a life cycle longer than two years, and obligingly come to vibrant life every spring for colour and beauty right through until winter.

Perennials used to be the mainstay of any garden, giving many of them nowadays the description "old-fashioned." Then came a time of rapid growth and change. People were on the move — living in new houses for several years and then relocating — and it seemed as if permanent gardens really were a thing of the past. Now it's changing back again. Many of us have decided to stay where we are for awhile and make the garden part of our home. And of course the easiest way to do this is to start planting flowers which will come up year after year with a minimum of fuss.

Perennials are not only colourful and interesting by themselves, they also provide a consistent backdrop for your favourite annuals. While they may seem to be more expensive when you first buy them, perennials can actually save you money in the long run because you don't have to keep buying them every year. They also spread out and provide new roots as they grow, so you can divide them up and replant in other parts of the garden.

There is nothing difficult about maintaining a perennial garden. Once you've planted the flowers properly, there is very little fussing around necessary — the plants just grow on their merry way.

However, a little knowledge about planning, buying and planting is necessary to guide you through the incredible variety of perennials. I have described some of the most popular perennial plants in this book, and given easy-to-follow directions on how to get them started and keep them healthy and productive year after year. I have also included a chapter on roses, listing the most outstanding and successful varieties and types, and setting down the simplest way to success.

Perennials will give you years of pleasure, and they illustrate the saying that, in garden beauty at least, everything old is new again.

Happy Gardening

Mark Cullen

Chapter One

Tools

Tools

Your won't need any special tools for creating and maintaining your perennial garden. The regular tools you would use for annual gardening and lawn care will usually be fine. The most important thing is that the quality of the tools be high. You're going to be using them as long as your garden grows, and with perennials that could be years. It's better to invest in the best tools you can at the start so you don't have to spend more money in the long run replacing cheap equipment. You should get tools made of tempered steel — forged rather than stamped.

You can often find good quality tools at garage sales and auctions at considerable savings. Any rust can be cleaned off with inexpensive rust removers, and your local hardware store can sharpen them if necessary. Buying tools new has advantages too. You know for sure that your are getting the best quality, and you get tools which are completely unworn.

Either way, if you are just starting out with a garden, you may find it a bit expensive to get everything all at once. Get the essentials first, and then keep adding the tools which will make gardening easier as you need them as you can afford them.

Care of Tools

Since you have spent a lot of money on them and want them to last a long time, if not forever, it makes sense to take good care of your tools.

- Give wooden handles a couple of coats of oil-based paint to protect them from the elements and make them easier to see in the garden.
- Have a place to store your tools which is easy to get to and close to the garden.

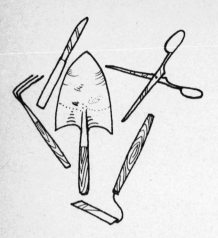

You don't need any specialized tools for perennial gardening — just the good quality equipment you'd use for other garden care.

- Hang tools up on nails or pegs to prevent damage and help keep them sharp.
- Clean tools after each use by dunking them in and out of oily sand. Just put some engine or other oil into a bucket of sand and keep it by the storage area where it will be handy. The oil will help prevent rust.
- Keep tools sharp. You can do this yourself or visit your local hardware store every once in a while.

Basic and Necessary

Shovel or Spade. One of these will be necessary for both planting and cultivating. A shovel has a spoon-like blade, whereas a spade can be useful because of its straight edge. Both are good but in a pinch, only one is necessary at first.

Trowel. You'll use the trowel to plant small perennials. Make sure it feels fairly heavy when you lift it up and that the handle fits your hand smoothly.

Garden Fork. You should have two of these to make dividing existing perennials easier. The fork is also good for gently turning in manure and fertilizer around existing plants without damaging the roots, and lifting and spreading leaf mold or other heavy mulch.

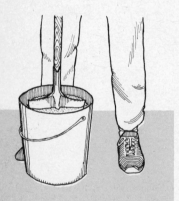

Keep tools clean the easy way by sliding them in and out of oily sand.

Wheelbarrow. You really can't do without a wheelbarrow in a large garden. It's the best thing for transporting tools, mulch and plants. There are many models available — many in light and durable plastic which doesn't rust. They may have one pneumatic tire or two rubber ones. If you plan on doing any really heavy work like carrying rocks or cement blocks for raised gardens or rock gardens, the sturdier steel models would probably be best.

Hose and Soaker. Perennials don't need a lot of watering, but when they do you should *soak* the earth — not water from above. This is especially true for roses. The best kind of hose is one which is 3/4" diameter because it carries more water. Attach it to a soaker hose which you can leave permanently in place in the flower bed.

Cultivator. The three curved prongs break up the earth around existing plants and can root out weeds. The smaller hand cultivator is useful around low-growing perennials.

Knife. You should have at least one good sharp knife for cutting through the woody stems of some perennials — whether you are cutting back dead blooms or picking flowers for the house. Make sure the knife has a rounded tip so you

A wheelbarrow is still the best thing to transport material and equipment around a big yard.

You'll find a good sharp knife to be a simple but effective tool. Make sure it has a round tip if you're going to carry it around in your back pocket.

Use a narrow rake to clean up under fully grown plants and shrubs and avoid tangles.

can carry it around with you without doing yourself an injury.

Rototiller. If you are just starting a new garden, you may need to use this to turn the earth over ... especially in a large or long bed. You can usually rent one quite easily.

Rake. You'll need a steel-tined rake to spread mulch and rake up debris in the fall. A narrow eight or ten inch one is better at getting under large plants and between rows.

Miscellaneous.

- strong gardening or leather gloves
- pH soil tester
- watering can
- twine
- tomato cages to support airy plants
- long 1″ square wooden stakes

Chapter Two

Materials

Materials

Since perennials usually stay where they are planted, the gardener doesn't get the chance to improve the soil all over again every year. It should as well prepared as possible before the plants go into the ground and there are many materials to help.

Soil Amendments

Almost all perennials do well in soil which is friable (light and crumbly), well-draining and nourishing. Organic materials, plant matter which was once alive and growing, can improve any soil except very heavy clay.

Peat Moss. This is the peat from bogs and marshes which is allowed to break down partially, then is dried and sold commercially. It is an excellent product for amending the soil. It has a natural affinity for moisture and holds water in the earth long enough for the roots to make good use of it. The important thing to remember about peat moss is that you should always dampen it before

Most perennials like soil which has been improved by adding organic materials like peat moss.

using. Never plant anything in earth with dry peat moss, or the moisture which should be going to the roots will go to the peat moss instead. This is an easily available and convenient product, and fine if you are only setting out a few plants, but if your are cultivating a large area you may want to consider a less expensive amendment.

Leaf Mold. Here is a time-honoured and inexpensive way to enrich your soil. Instead of throwing away the fallen leaves of autumn, use them in your garden instead. Many lawn mowers now have shredders attached, and you can dig these shredded leaves right into the

Make your own leaf mold by packing leaves into black plastic bags for the winter.

ground in the fall. To make good leaf mold from unshredded leaves, just put them into heavy black plastic bags, dampen them and pack them down, then put the bags in a place where they will get the winter sun. By spring, the leaves will have broken down enough to go into the earth. You can also get leaf mold at the nursery if you don't have any trees.

Manure. An excellent amendment for the earth and, since the plant materials have been obligingly broken down by the insides of an animal, for the gardener too. You can buy both sheep and cattle manure at gardening centres. The most important thing about manure is that it be sterilized and free from weed seeds before you add it to the earth. Otherwise you may find yourself with the best garden of weeds in the neighbourhood.

Compost. This is a general term used for plant material which has broken down into crumbly tilth. It aerates the soil, adds nutrients, and generally enriches the soil. You can buy commercially composted material at the nursery, or produce your own using the methods for The Compost Bin and The Super Composter which I have described in my book "ANNUALS".

Ammonium Sulphate. If you are adding an amendement like peat moss or compost which is fully broken down, you probably won't have to add nitrogen. However, if you are using shredded leaves or other material which will continue to decay in the earth, you will need to add extra nitrogen as well. Otherwise the material will steal nitrogen from the earth around it to help in the breaking down process and you don't want that. Amendments you buy at the nursery should have "nitrogen fortified" written on the bags. If not, or if you are adding partially composted material of your own, mix in some ammonium sulphate, or something similar which your gardening centre can recommend, at the rate of one ounce per square yard.

Bone Meal. This is something many perennial gardeners swear by, particularly when planting roses and dahlias. It is high in phosphate and contains some nitrogen, but it is also fairly expensive so a handful thrown into the planting hole itself is the most economical way of using it.

Gypsum. Clay soils are greatly improved by the addition of gypsum. Dig it in at the rate of one ounce per foot to help the soil drain more efficiently.

Buy a commercial fertilizer with a low first (nitrogen) number, and a high middle (potassium) number.

Commercial Fertilizer. As well as organic amendments which feed the plants through the soil, there are commercial fertilizers available at your local nursery. Generally, perennials like those which are low in nitrogen. The numbers on the front of the fertilizer package refer to the three main elements in the order of nitrogen, phosphorous and potassium. Get one with a low first number, as too much nitrogen when the plant is growing will encourage leaves — not blooms.

Mulch. This is the layer of material you put on top of the earth to keep the roots cool, the weeds down, and the moisture constant. You can use attractive and effective materials like wood chips and gravel, or organic materials like compost and manure which will enrich the earth as they break down. Pine needles are excellent if you have them around, as are grass clippings as long as they haven't been sprayed with anything. Straw, fir boughs and leaves can be used in the winter after the ground has frozen, and leaf mold is good in the spring.

Chapter Three

Planning the Garden

Planning The Garden

Planning is one of the most important parts of planting perennials. Time spent learning about your plants before you put them in the ground can often be the deciding factor in success or failure. Because perennial borders in the past were often planned and planted by professional gardeners on large estates, some of us are a bit daunted by the idea of creating any kind of perennial garden. This is unnecessary since we are the masters of our own backyards. We can decide whether we want just one or two perennials planted every year, or a whole bed planted at once. We can also breath easier knowing that once we've given them a good start, perennials will forge ahead and do their part too.

Paper Planning

Putting pencil to paper is almost as necessary in creating a garden as putting a spade into earth. Write down the nature of the garden you want and what you have to work with-taking into consideration the following.

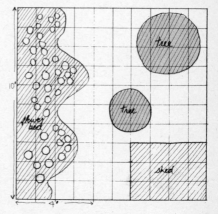

Planting a beautiful garden is easier if you make a plan on paper first.

Space and Shape. Pace out the area of the entire garden and the spaces of any existing beds (each pace being a foot), and make a drawing showing the measurements. Graph paper is excellent for this. Indicate any slopes and hills, and existing shrubs and perennials — also places where you prefer to plant annuals.

Sun and Shade. Note on the drawing any areas which are in complete shade or total sunlight. In other areas, note the type of light received (filtered sunlight, partial shade, morning or afternoon sun) and indicate by shadings on the paper or initials. The growing season is the best time to discover this.

Viewing Points. Decide where the garden will be seen from most often. This is important in design. If you will be seeing it from one end of the garden — from the back of the house, for example — you will plant differently than if you were going to be viewing it directly from a central patio.

Formal or Informal. A formal garden is detailed and symetrical. It is nice for small areas which are straight-lined and flat. The basic rectangular shape is easy to lay out and take care of. An informal garden usually contains a greater variety of flower colours and shapes, and the edge of the border may be deeply scalloped. This creates depth and visual interest since the brighly coloured plants can be put in the front and literally thrust out into the garden.

Beds or Borders. Beds are like islands of earth surrounded by a sea of grass or gravel. They can be created in the ground or made into raised gardens. When you're planning, you should take into consideration the fact that, to look its best, a bed should have at least two to three times its own size all around it. If you can accomplish this, there are several advantages to creating a perennial bed — even a small one.

A border with deeply scalloped edges creates visual interest and is fun to plant.

1. Beds are eye-catching and can be viewed from all angles.

2. They get good air circulation which cuts down on disease.
3. Depending on where you put them, they will receive more sunlight.
4. Beds are easy to look after since you can cultivate them from all sides.
5. If you construct a raised bed, you will continue to have proper drainage year after year.

A bed is like an island of flowers surrounded by a sea of grass.

Borders have always been the most popular gardens. They are exactly what they sound like — areas which border the edges. When planning, remember that the depth of a border (or the combined depths of borders on either side) should only be one quarter the width of the yard. Even in a very large area, the borders should be less than five feet deep if they are up against a wall or fence, so you can take care of them properly. There are several advantages to borders.

1. They leave a large block of space in the middle of the garden. This is important in smaller yards where you don't want things to look crowded.
2. If they are placed at the edge against a fence or wall, the wind will be less damaging to taller perennials.
3. They hide or soften the sight of those walls and

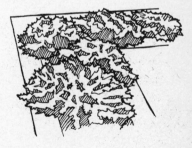

A border is still the most popular kind of perennials garden.

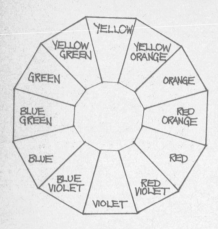

The colour wheel can show you warm colours (from yellow over to orange) and the cool colours (violet over to green).

fences, as well as providing a frame for the lawn.
4. Borders can also be raised up from the ground using attractive edgings in various heights like railway ties, or mini-walls of bricks or stone.

Progressive Planting

Once you've decided what kind of flowers you want, it may not be practical or possible for you to plant them all in one season. Print the names of the flowers on your chart where you eventually want them to grow, and use different colours of ink to denote year one, year two and so on. As time goes by, you may

decide to change some aspects of your drawings, but you will always have the original plan to work from.

Choosing the Plants

There are four basic things to consider when deciding what flowers to plant in your perennial garden: colour, height, spread, and time of bloom.

Colour

A colour wheel gives only the most basic colours, but it can show which ones are warm and which ones are cool. From yellow over to orange is considered warm, and from violet over to green is considered cool. Red-violet and yellow-green can be considered both.

The warm colours seem to come toward you in the garden, so they can make a large rambling area seem more intimate. If you plant them in a garden which is further away — at the bottom of the lawn, for instance — that place will seem closer and come into sharp focus. Massed, warm colours provide drama, and because they draw the eye, act as accent points in the border.

The cool colours seem to recede. They can make a small garden seem cooler and larger. When you plant them in the border, they add depth to that spot. They are particularly good for gardens which are seen close up, because at a distance, they just seem to fade away.

Warm and cool colours can be used together for interesting degrees of depth and drama as long as you remember that too many warm colours can easily overpower the quieter cool ones.

Hues, Tints and Shades. Within the general colour you've chosen will be variations called hues, tints and shades.

- A pure colour is a hue.
- A lighter version of that colour is a tint.
- A darker version is a shade.

You can plant a stretch or even a whole garden with the hues, tints and shades of one colour. This is not only easy, but it also creates a dramatic and harmonious effect.

Three Colour Planting. Choose a colour you like which is either warm or cool. Look on the colour wheel and find the ones on each side of your chosen colour. Then plan your garden with these three colours and their various tints and shades. Three colour planting is very popular and effective.

Complimentary Colour Planting. Choose colours which are opposite on the colour wheel. This works best with plants

Height is important in choosing plants. Usually the tallest are put at the back and the short at the front.

that have good strong hues — not shades or tints. In this kind of planting, white is very effective. It both enhances and calms down the highly dramatic effect of complimentary colours, and creates a wonderful glow at dusk.

Height

Height is particularly important in a perennial garden as some of these plants can grow up to six feet or more. The most practical way of deciding on plants for a border is to start with short plants at the front, and work up to the tallest at the their neighbours. The trick is to find out what the average and desirable spread is, and then plan and plant accordingly.

Time of Bloom

Most perennials have their own particular time of bloom, and usually this lasts for only a couple of weeks. When planning your garden, you'll probably want to have different plants which will bloom in succession so you'll always have something new and colourful in the garden. Very soon you'll start looking forward to the time each flower is at its peak — from peonies to chrysanthemums — as punctuation points in the growing season. This can bring even an inner city gardener closer to the rhythms of nature.

Cutting Garden

Many perennials are wonderful for cutting and using in arrangements so you can bring the beauty of your garden indoors. If you have a suitable spot, create a garden which will grow flowers specifically for this purpose.

A cutting garden is simple and practical. The flowers should be planted in rows similar to vegetables in a vegetable garden. Put planks between these rows so you can walk through the flowers without packing down the earth and

If you have space you can create a garden just to grow flowers for cutting and putting into arrangements.

back. Raised or middle-of-the-garden beds can either have all plants approximately the same height, or use the graduated principle with the tallest in the middle.

The garden shouldn't look too rigid though. The purpose is to keep the flowers from being totally hidden from view — not create a staircase.

Spread

With perennials, this is almost as important as height. Some can just gallop along, spreading like mad and crowding out retarding root growth. You can lay the garden out anywhere — even in a spot which is not part of the main landscaping area — as long as it will get at least 4 to 6 hours of sun every day. Another use for cutting gardens is as a home "nursery" to grow plants which can later be transplanted to borders or beds.

Chapter Four

Planting the Garden

Planting The Garden

Whether you are preparing to set out a few plants or establishing a whole new bed, the most important part of the process is preparing the soil. Think of the soil as the home your plants will be living in for the rest of their lives. It should be light enough to support tall inhabitants. It should be able to hold moisture long enough to give the plants enough water, but loose enough to let the water drain away so the roots don't drown from lack of oxygen. This underground home should also be rich in elements which will feed the hungry plants and keep them healthy and beautiful.

Creating this environment is similar to the definition of genius — ten percent inspiration and ninety percent perpiration. Gardening is one occupation, however, where this effort is completely enjoyable, and the results even more so.

Preparing the Soil

The soil for perennials should be prepared about one month before planting. This gives the earth a chance to become aerated, and the organic amendments time to break down and mix in.

In temperate parts of the country, some plants can be set out in the fall, but in most of the cold-winter areas, it's best to wait until spring so that young plants don't get winter-killed before they have a chance to take hold.

In the Fall

In established beds, clear away debris and pull any withered annuals out of the place intended for your perennials. Turn the soil over and add shredded leaves or compost.

If you are creating a new bed, cut out the shape you want and

When you prepare the earth for planting, remember that it will be the home your flowers will be living in.

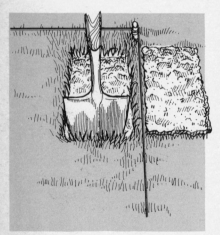

When creating a new bed or border, chop the sod up and turn it under.

turn the sod under — chopping it up with a spade so it will decompose faster.

Cover the bed with leaves, straw or other fluffy mulch so the earth will be warmer earlier in the spring and easier to work.

In the Spring

As soon as the soil can be worked in the spring, rake off the mulch and turn the soil over to the depth of your spade. Crumble any large pieces of sod by rubbing it between your hands. Any unmanageable bits can be put in the compost bin.

Spade in your organic material — peat moss, manure, leaf mold or compost. Don't stint. You should put one third to one half of the amount of earth. If you're cultivating down twelve inches put four to six inches of compost on top and spade it in. There's no point in spending good money for plants and then holding back on the very soil amendments which will feed and cultivate those plants.

After you have done all this to the soil, wait at least a month before planting. This will give the amendments time to mingle with the earth. It will also give the soil time to warm up. You should never put a tender plant into cold ground, so test the soil to see if it is warm enough. Simply pick up a handful and squeeze it. If it feels at all cold, wait. When you can pick up a handful and hold it without feeling any chill, then you'll know it's time to plant.

Large Borders

It can be back-breaking to cultivate large borders by hand. If you want to create a new bed or border on a large scale, it would be a good idea to use power digging. You can rent a rototiller at most gardening centres.

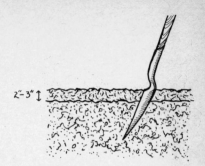

Don't be stingy when adding organic amendments to the soil.

— Prepare the earth the same way you would for hand digging — removing debris and weeds.
— Make sure the soil is damp enough to be soft, but definitely not wet.
— Go over the area thoroughly with the rototiller.
— Put your amendments on top of the turned earth and then go over it again. Don't overdo it. There is a tendency with power cultivators to go at it again and again. However, the amendments won't do as much good if they are broken in too finely.
— Rake smooth and leave for at least a month or until the soil is warm to the touch before planting.

Acid and Alkaline Soils

Most perennials are perfectly happy in soil which is normal to

Before planting in the spring, make sure the soil is warm to the touch.

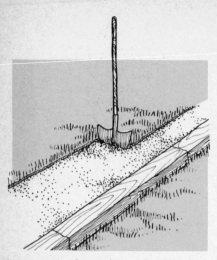

For raised gardens, build supports of stones, bricks or railways ties, and fill with amended earth.

slightly acid on the pH scale — 6.5 to 7.0. The term pH stands for potential hydrogen, and measures the acid and alkaline properties of the earth. You can buy a pH testing kit at your gardening centre, and test the soil yourself. If your soil is very alkaline, peat moss added to the soil will bring the level down to normal. If you want a bed which will suit alkaline loving plants you can add limestone. Sprinkle it on top of the earth until it covers it completely and then work it in. This should give you a good alkaline level.

You should do this in the fall or early spring so the amendments have time to work before you plant.

Raised Beds

Dig out the sod, if necessary, and put the top six inches of topsoil in a wheelbarrow. Do this in sections. Lay the sod, green side down, in the dug-out area. Mix the topsoil with peat moss and enough commercial topsoil, potting soil and even vermiculite to fill the built-up area (surrounded with bricks, boards or railways ties) with good friable earth.

Deep Borders

You can have borders deeper than five feet if you have a large space and if you leave some room at the back of the border which is big enough for a plank of wood. This will allow you to get at the garden from the back. The flowers will hide the space and the air circulation will also be better.

Before Planting

Transfer Plan. After the earth has been prepared and just before planting, start to transfer the plan you made on paper into the garden itself. Put the names of the plants you have chosen on flat marker sticks and poke these into the bed or border to correct distance apart. When you buy your plants, you'll know exactly where to put them.

Buying Plants. If you're planning on developing a large border, or want to see your plants grow right from the beginning, you might want to start your perennial seeds yourself. (See the chapter on propagation in my book "Houseplants".)

However, you'll get a headstart if you buy from a nursery as these young plants already have at least one season's growth. Potted perennials are expensive but you'll be able to see what you're getting. Visit the nursery in the spring and early summer as this is the time when they will be in bloom. You'll be able to see the colours and get an idea of what they will look like when they're grown.

Get a headstart on your flowers' growth by buying young plants at the nursery — either in pots or six-packs.

Look for plants which are bushy and full — never leggy. If you know exactly what you want and don't have to see the colour before you buy, look for plants with good green leaves and no blooms.

If you are prepared to wait another year for any significant growth, you can save money by buying one-year growth perennials in six-packs. You can also buy perennials from a catalogue at considerable savings. Decide what you want during the long cold days of winter, and send in your order according to your updated plan on paper.

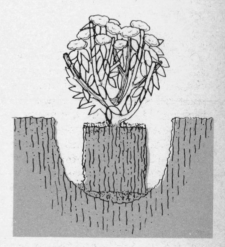

The plants should arrive at the right time for planting in your area, but they will arrive dry-rooted — that is, not

When transfering a plant from a container, dig a hole twice as big as the rootball.

Be as gentle as possible with young plants and ease them out of their containers.

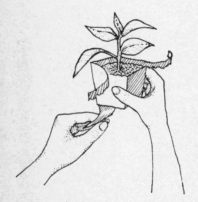

Cut off the top and bottom of the peat pot and put the rest in the ground with the plant.

planted in earth. They are usually wrapped in spaghum moss and plastic. If you can't set them out right away, or if the weather isn't suitable or the earth warm enough, simply moisten the moss and keep the plants in a cool dark place still wrapped in the plastic. You should transplant as soon as possible after this, although the plants will be all right for a week or two.

Planting the Plants. Container plants have many live sensitive roots which can suffer shock when they leave their nice familiar home and are put into a strange hole in the ground. This is one of the reasons why you should make sure the earth is fully prepared and warm before transplanting.

Another way you can reduce trauma is to water the plant while it is still in the pot about an hour before setting out. Add a cup of double-diluted fertilizer low in nitrogen like Plant Start 5-15-5.

Dig a hole about twice the size of the rootball, and deep enough so that the top of the earth on the ball will be just under the soil line.

If the plant is in a plastic container, loosen the earth around the sides with a flat knife. Then turn the pot on its side, tap the bottom, and gently ease the plant out of the container.

If the container is made of

metal, ask the nurseryman to make cuts down two sides. When you are ready to plant, pull the sides down carefully and remove the entire rootball, getting as much damp earth as possible.

Six-pack youngsters can be pushed out by pressing your thumbs on the bottom of the container, and if you have plants which have been grown in peat pots, cut off the part at the top which comes above the soil, and remove the bottom. The rest of the peat should decompose in the earth, adding extra nutrients.

The one thing to remember about getting your plants out of whatever container they're in is: DON'T PULL. Ease them out. These are living things and they won't respond well if they're yanked.

Once the plants are out of the pots, they should be put into the ground immediately. Place them in the proper-sized hole with a handful of damp peat moss for good measure, and very gently rub the rootball to spread out the roots. Fill halfway up with earth and tamp this down with your foot. Continue filling and tamping until the soil lines are even, then water thoroughly. This will get rid of any air pockets which could cause damage to the roots.

Dormant or dry-rooted plants look almost dead when you get them, as if they'll never grow or

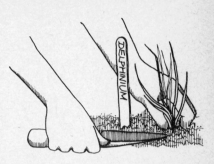

Place marker sticks beside newly planted flowers.

bloom. Don't panic. This is the way they are supposed to look.

When you are ready to set out, take the plants out of the plastic bags, shake off the moss, and put the roots into lukewarm water for an hour. (Keep the tags on the stems so you don't get confused.) Make sure the earth is fully prepared and finely textured, then dig a shallow hole, large enough for the roots, and loosen the earth in the bottom.

Take the plants out of the water and cut off any broken or damaged parts. The roots should be plumped up now. If they're not, you can send the plant back and ask for a replacement, assuming that you've treated it properly since it arrived.

Gently spread the roots out in the bottom of the hole and fill halfway up with earth. Tamp with your foot, and fill up to the top. Tamp again and water thoroughly. Don't add fertilizer. Replace your marker stick and check the plant off on your written plan.

Don't let the small size of the new plants convince you to put them closer together than you planned on paper. You may think the poor little things look forlorn and lonely all by themselves, but don't give in to temptation and plant neighbours too close. In no time at all, those poor little plants will be lush and fully spread grownups, and will need all the space you originally thought they would for light, nutrients and water.

Chapter Five

Plant Care

Plant Care

While perennials don't need to be coddled, they do need a certain amount of care. A healthy environment will help prevent disease, and a little attention every once in a while will keep your garden growing beautifully.

Watering

If you have an adequate summer rainfall, additional watering isn't necessary. You may get the occasional dry spell when it would be a good idea to get the hose out and give everything a soaking, but otherwise perennials will thrive on the bounty of nature.

In an area where the summers are hot and dry, the matter is a bit different. Then you should water deeply at ground level at least once a week. Don't water heavily from the top as the flowers may get heavy and break off. You must always *soak* the ground under the plants because if you water lightly, you'll encourage the roots to grow up toward the surface

When perennials need water, give it to them from underneath. A soaker hose makes it easy.

where they can get scorched by the heat of the sun. Water plants so the soil is damp at least four inches down. Use a soaker hose for convenience.

If you need to water, the best time to do it is in the morning or at least five hours before sundown. Although you should keep the foliage as dry as possible (to discourage fungus diseases and burning from the sun) you may want to freshen the leaves up with a little gentle shower sometimes. Pick a morning when it is not too hot or windy and use a fine spray.

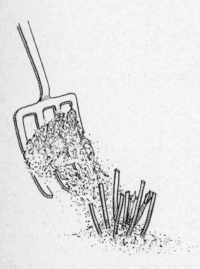

Mulch is the silent caretaker of your garden, but don't let it crowd the stems of your plants.

Fertilizing

In the spring, put some composted and weed-free manure around the base of the plant and work it into the soil with a gardening fork, twisting it gently so the roots aren't disturbed. Then at the beginning of May, June, and July, you can augment this feeding with a small amount of slow release granular fertilizer. Make sure it has a low first number (low in nitrogen) and a high second number (high in phosphorous). Look for the numbers 5-10-5 or something similar. It's important that you don't put too much nitrogen into the earth around your perennials as this will stimulate the growth of foliage at the expense of flowers.

Don't fertilize after midsummer as this will encourage growth which might be winterkiller.

Mulching

This is a very important part of plant care. Mulch is the materials (peat moss, compost, bark chips, pine needles), which you put on top of the earth to do an on-going job of taking care of the plants. It keeps down weeds, keeps roots cool, prevents fungus spores from flying up onto leaves, and maintains a good moisture balance.

Sometimes the mulch around perennials can get crusty

because the soil isn't constantly replanted and cultivated the way it is in annual and vegetable gardens. This is particularly true if you use peat moss. Make sure you occasionally break up the mulch with a gardening fork or cultivator so the rain can get into the ground.

The mulch should be spread about two inches thick everywhere except right around the stem. Here it should taper off to one inch or less, as too much mulch around the stems can encourage chewing insects.

Staking

Two kinds of plants need staking so they don't flop over — single stalked plants like delphinium, and those with many stems like carnations and chrysanthemums. Green bamboo poles, which you can buy in large packets, are excellent for the first kind. As the plant grows up, fasten it to the pole (which should be pushed firmly into the ground) with green plastic twist ties. Get the material which comes in a role so you can cut off exactly what you need. Or use green twine. The second kind of floppy plants have always called for more complicated staking methods, but now we have the tomato cage which makes everything much easier. Put the cage over the plant when it is small. As it grows, the branches will come

Put tomato cages over floppy plants before they start to grow.

through the wire and eventually hide it completely. At the same time, the plant will be supported and yet look natural.

To Prevent Heaving

Any place in Canada which is not in a reliably temperate zone is subject to winter frost. Since perennials stay in the ground over the winter, they are particularly susceptible to heaving.

This is what happens when the ground freezes, then thaws, then freezes again. The ground literally heaves up. This can cause cracking in roads and sidewalks and uneveness in lawns. In the perennial garden, it can sometimes force the plants right up out of the ground.

To prevent this, you should mulch heavily in the late fall but after the ground has experienced several good frosts. If you lay out nice warm material too soon, you're apt to encourage large families of mice and other nesting rodents, which will happily dine on the roots and stems of your flowers. If the ground is frozen down a couple of inches before you mulch, your roots should be safe.

The mulch you use to prevent heaving should be large and

Don't put winter mulch on your plants too soon or you'll encourage mice to dine on tender roots.

airy. Pine branches are excellent if you have some from pruning. Raking on dry leaves is an inexpensive and time-honoured method. Straw is favored by many gardeners, but make sure your timing is right because mice just love this stuff.

Dividing

There are some perennials which get to a certain size and stay that way year after year. There are also some which just keep spreading. Like business and industry, they seem to feel that their entire purpose is to expand and grow. If left unattended, these pervasive perennials can cause damage to other plants and adversely affect their own health. As they form bigger clumps every year, they compete for nutrients and water with others. Eventually they start to deteriorate in the centre as their outer growth steals these nutrients from the inner and older growth. The plants can then literally starve to death due to their own rapid growth. The gardener can help by dividing the plants up.

When to Divide. Plants which bloom in the spring and summer, like peonies, should be divided in the fall. Plants which bloom in the fall, like chrysanthemums, should be divided in the srping. If the winters are

very cold where you live, ignore
these rules and do all your dividing in the spring or early
summer.

You don't necessarily have to
divide every plant every year,
but if you start to feel that
you're being overtaken by an
army of iris, it's time to get out
the spade and fork and get to
work.

How To Divide.

- Cut the plants down to six
  inches from the ground.
- The day before dividing,
  water the earth thoroughly.

*Stubborn root clumps can be
separated for replanting with
two garden forks.*

- Dig out the entire clump and
  put it on a canvas sheet or
  plastic garbage bag.
- Discard any dead parts, and
  divide the healthy part of the
  clump into smaller clumps.
  Sometimes a clump will be so
  tangled that it seems impos-
  sible to separate. Cutting it
  up can cause root damage.
  The best way to get it apart is
  to insert two gardening forks
  into the middle of the clump,
  both facing outward. Take a
  handle in each hand and push
  them apart — then back and
  forth. The tines of the forks
  will eventually separate the
  clump into useable parts
  which haven't been damaged.
- Enrich the hole with a fertilizer which is very low in nitrogen or has none at all.
  Replant some of the clumps
  in this hole and backfill —

*Use a three-pronged cultivator
to loosen weeds out of awkward
places.*

tamping the earth down with your foot. Water.

- Replant the other clumps in new locations in your own garden, give them to friends, or discard them.

Grooming

Walk around your garden every couple of days with a knife and a small basket or container for debris. Cut off any dead or withered blooms.

Keep the ground under the plants clean by picking up fallen leaves or blossoms. These can harbour chewing insects and encourage disease.

A fungicid like Funginex will prevent and treat mildew and black spot disease.

Weeds should be mercifully rare if you've kept the earth well-mulched. If and when you happen to see a weed, get it out immediately and be sure to dig up the root. A knife is good for small jobs, and a cultivator for awkward places. Remember that weeds are thieves which can quickly rob the earth of nutrients and moisture.

If you see any sign of disease on your plants, remove the damaged part immediately and put it in a plastic garbage bag. Never put it in the compost bin or in a pile at the corner of the garden. Spores can often live for two seasons and infect other plants.

Loosen the soil around your perennials every once in a while with a cultivator or garden fork. This will give the plants some air and let moisture in, but do this gently so you don't damage the roots.

Grass can be a big problem if it gets a hold of the earth around perennials. When it gets very bad, dig up the clump, pull out the grass and grass roots, and then quickly put the plant back in the ground.

In the fall, cut down dead and woody stalks. Dispose of them or cut them up and put them on the compost pile. Do a general clean-up before putting on any airy mulch for the winter, by raking up debris and pulling out any weeds or dead annuals. Otherwise you'll just be encouraging whole colonies of pests.

Pests and Diseases

Perennials are happily healthy. When the gardener practices good grooming, watering, and mulching procedures there is little chance of illness.

If you see any sign of black spot (a fungus disease where the leaves have black spots and turn yellow) you should remove the diseased parts and treat the rest of the plant with a fungicide like Funginex.

If, in spite of your best efforts you have a problem, ask an expert — either at your local nursery or at a local government office.

Chapter Six

Roses

Roses

As the poet Gertrude Stein once observed: "A rose is a rose is a rose." So varied is the beauty of our most popular flower that it often defies description. Roses have long been the symbols of love and romance, as well as the darlings of professional gardeners and enthusiastic amateurs. Many books have been written on roses and how to grow them. Sometimes this can be a bit daunting to someone who would just like to start out with a few well-chosen bushes and see some success, without making it too difficult or complicated. However, this is not only possible but fully within your grasp as long as you observe a few simple guidelines for choosing, planting and pruning. Then, with a moderate amount of care, you can make beautiful roses one of the highlights of your garden.

What Roses Want

As with any new venture, it's wise to have a plan before going out and buying a lot of rose bushes. You should take into consideration where you want your roses to grow and where they will do their best. Perhaps you want to start slowly with a few bushes in an existing border, or perhaps you want to use them alone along a front walkway. Here are some things to keep in mind.

Sunshine. Roses need at least six hours of sunshine every day for the best blooms. Be very careful to check this out before planting them next to a north or south wall.

Good Drainage. This is essential. Roses should be deeply watered so the roots will stay down in the cool ground, but the water must be allowed to drain away or the plants will drown.

Air Circulation. One of the reasons professional gardeners often plant roses in separate beds (away from walls and other flowers) is so they will get a proper amount of air moving around them. Without this, even the healthiest rose could easily get black spot or mildew which any gardener wants to avoid. On the other hand, you shouldn't plant your roses where they will have to battle prevailing winds. A good compromise will keep the fruits of your hard work as healthy as possible.

Room For Roots. Roses not only need room enough to spread out on top, but under the ground as well. Planting them too near trees and shrubs can cause trouble. The pervasive and hungry roots of these neighbours gobble up important nutrients and moisture which the roses need.

What You Want

In planning your rose display, you should have some idea of what you eventually want — whether you are simply contemplating one bush to start out with, or making roses the focal point of the garden. Roses can be divided into several basic types — each with its own unique characteristics. These will determine whether the blooms will be single or in a cluster, and what shape the bush will be. Once you have decided, it's a good idea to get some help from the experts at the nursery to

Plant roses where they will get lots of room, away from the hungry roots of neighbours.

make sure you're getting exactly what you want.

Hybrid Teas. Many people think these are the loveliest of all the roses. Long slender buds turn into luxuriant single blooms with outstanding colours and a beautiful scent. The fact that they are also excellent cut roses makes them even more popular.

Floribundas. These have clusters of flowers in a wide variety of colours. This type forms a wonderful display in any context — whether as a single plant, massed together to form an edging or hedge, or as part of an established rose garden. They are usually hardy and bloom right through the growing season.

Grandifloras. This class of rose combines the attributes of both the Hybrid Teas and the Floribundas. There are still clusters but they are formed of Hybrid Tea-like blooms. This is an excellent type of rose for the beginner as it blooms in profusion and is easy to grow.

Climbers. These are great fun and provide a spectacular effect. A good spread of climbing roses can add real beauty to your home as well as covering what may have been a boring wall. You can also use them over rounded arbors leading

Beautiful Hybrid Tea roses are among the most popular because of their stunning colours and scents.

into the back garden, against fences and on trellises.

Experience and interest can lead the gardener to other types of rose. Whatever your preference, your local nursery will have expert help and plenty of full-colour pictures to help you in your selection.

Choosing Roses

When buying Hybrid Teas, you should always get ones which have been developed for life in Canada. This type of rose has the top grafted onto the roots. The ones best suited for the harshness of our winters have

When you discover that the basics of rose growing are so easy and rewarding, you may want to move on to other types of roses — like the tree rose.

Climbing roses can add spectacular beauty to your home — on walls, arbors or fences.

hardy rootstalks, whereas some of the varieties available from the enormous growing centres in California haven't. Although new Hybrid Teas are being developed all the time, here are some of the ones which have proved themselves in performance and popularity over the years. Most Hybrid Teas grow from 3 to 4 feet.

Crimson Glory — Dark velvety red with a deep memorable fragrance.
Chrysler Imperial — Deep red with a heavy fragrance.
Tropicana — Orange-red with a heavy fragrance.
Peace — Yellow blend with a heavy fragrance.
Tiffany — Pink blend with a heavy fragrance.

Floribundas are grown on their own rootstalk so any you buy in your district will be fine for your particular climate. Popular varieties, which usually grow up to 3 feet, are:

Fashion — Pink blend with a light fragrance.
Carousel — Deep red with a good fragrance.
Circus — Yellow, red and pink with a good fragrance.

The colours of the Grandiflora roses are just as varied as the Hybrid Teas. Ask for new varieties as well as old favourites.

These roses usually grow 3 to 4 feet.

Queen Elizabeth — Medium pink with a good fragrance. (over 4 feet)
Golden Girl — Medium yellow with a good fragrance.
Camelot — Salmon-coral with a good fragrance.
John Armstrong — Dark red with a good fragrance.

Climbing roses can be either Hybrid Teas or Floribunda so make sure you know what you're getting before you buy.

Blaze — Outstanding crimson colour with a good fragrance.
White Dawn — White with a good fragrance.
New Dawn — Pink with a good fragrance.
High Noon — Yellow with a good fragrance.
Crimson Glory — Crimson with a heavy fragrance.

Preparing the Soil

A little preparation before planting will guarantee years of success, and make setting the roses into the earth much faster and easier. Timing is important. In temperate climates, it's possible to plant roses in the fall for early spring growth, but where the winters are more severe, it is usually safer to do it in the spring. When you have decided on your type of rose and its loca-

tion, turn that soil over to the depth of the spade. To this loosened soil, add one-third to one-half as much again of composted humus like leaf mold, peat moss, or composted manure. You should do this in the early spring as soon as the ground can be worked and at least a month before you plant the roses. This will allow the air and warmth to get at the soil, and the compost to break down. Roses like a fairly acid soil (about 7.0 pH) and you can check this very easily with a pH soil tester. If you know you have an alkaline soil, you might be

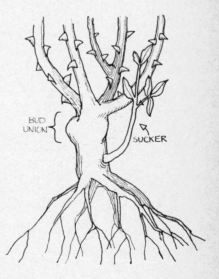

Bare root roses look dead when you get them, but they're not.

better off creating a raised garden for your roses, or you can also add an acid-released fertilizer (prepared for azaleas) to the existing earth.

Preparing the Roses

These are two ways of buying roses for planting: bare-root and potted.

Bare-Root. These come, as the name suggests, with bare roots and a short amount of cane above. (To the uninitiated, they often look dead, but a good soaking will prove otherwise.)

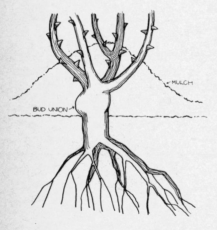

Plant bud union just above the soil line to encourage new cane growth, then mound with earth in the fall to prevent winter-kill.

As soon as you get them, remove from the plastic casing and cut off any broken or overly long roots.

If you can't plant them right away, put them back into the plastic wrap along with dampened moss or peat moss and store in a cool, dry place for up to a week.

When you're ready to plant, soak the roots in luke-warm water for an hour until they have plumped up. If they don't plump up at all, send them back to the nursery as they won't do anything in the ground.

Potted. Roses which have been started in containers by the nurseries have several advantages. They have a head-start on growth — displaying the colour and shape of the blooms in certain cases — and can show immediate progress. However, they are also considerably more expensive than bare-root roses, so the choice can sometimes be made on that basis alone. They need very little preparation. Simply water them well an hour or two before planting, and then make two complete slits down the sides of the container just before putting into the ground.

Setting Out

For years there has been disagreement about how deep to plant roses in cold winter climates. Ideally the bud union (the large bulbous part between the canes and the roots) should be above the ground to encourage new cane growth. However, if the bud union gets damaged by the cold, that's the end of the rose. As a result, many people have made a practice of planting the bud union under the ground. A practical compromise has been reached which is now used by many gardeners. Simply plant the rose bush so that the bud union is just above the soil line, and then cover it over with earth, before the cold weather comes, to protect it from the cold.

With bare-root roses, you should dig a hole deep enough so that the bud union will be in the right place. Dig the hole to fit the direction the roots are growing in — either spread out in a circle or all going out to the same side — and loosen the earth at the bottom of the hole. Then mix it with a spadeful of peat moss and a handful of bonemeal. If the roots are fanned out, you can make a mound at the bottom of the hole for the roots to spread over. Put the dampened plants into the hole and spread the roots out with your fingers so they aren't tangled or wound around the stem. Then carefully backfill to halfway up the hole with the earth you previously removed. Tamp this down very gently with your foot, then fill the hole with water and leave

for an hour. Tamp down again. This will get rid of any air-pockets which would be harmful to the growing rose. Fill up to the soil line, tamp and water again, and then mound any remaining earth up around the canes. This will keep everything moist and protected until the plant has started to grow. After a month, level the earth down to the soil line again.

With container roses, you should dig the hole about twice as big as the earth ball. Prepare the bottom of the hole the same

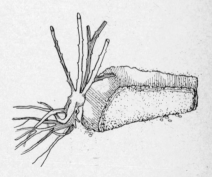

When planting dry root roses, dig a hole which fits the direction of the roots.

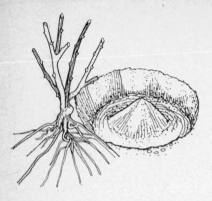

Where the roots naturally grow in a circle, mound the earth up in the hole and spread the the roots over.

way as for bare-root planting without any mounding. Make sure that the bud union will be just above the soil line when the rose is planted. Pull the sides of the container away from the earth ball. If the container is made of peat, many experts believe you can just plant the rose in the slit container and let the peat dissolve into the earth with time. However, if you prefer to remove the rose from the container, tap it on the bottom with a trowel and go round the inside with a knife to loosen the earth. Ease the rose out and place it immediately in the hole. Continue with the planting method for bare-root roses, including mounding the earth around the canes for a time.

Watering

Roses are ladies who don't like to get their leafy clothes wet. This means you should always water from underneath, soaking the earth until it is damp but not soggy. Drops of water on the leaves can cause burning, and lead to black spot disease.

It's better to water thoroughly once a week than lightly several times in the same period. Give roses too much water, though, and they'll drown. The best time to water is in the morning or at least 4 to 5 hours before dusk so that any excess moisture can be absorbed by the heat of the day.

Soak the soil underneath roses but don't get the leaves wet.

Mulching

Roses like moisture and they like it consistently without either going dry or drowning from overwatering. One way to ensure that the soil around the roots will always be cool and damp is to mulch with a good organic material like home-made humus, leaf mold or peat moss, or longer-lasting materials like pine bark chips when you've decided on the mulch you want, use it constantly. As well as keeping the soil moist, mulch can also keep down black spot disease. You see, when drops of water hit the bare earth, they can send up the spores of the black spot fungus which then settle on the underside of the leaves. They develop into little black spots and eventually the leaves turn yellow. The mulch will help prevent black spot but if you do happen to find any leaves in this condition pick them off and burn them right away, or put them in a plastic garbage bag away from other plants. Then lay down fresh mulch and dust the leaves with Funginex.

Feeding

You should feed about three times during the growing season — at the ends of May, June and July. (Don't feed in August as this will encourage growth which will only get winter-

Pine bark chips make a good mulch which is also attractive.

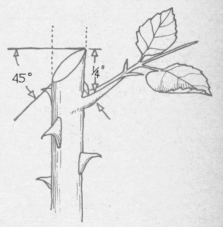

When cutting or pruning roses, always make a sharp cut at a 45' angle just above an outward facing bud.

killed.) Feed with a solution of Rose Food 3-9-8 at the rate of one cup per plant. Professional growers use a trick to get dark-green glossy leaves. All they do is put a cup of Epsom salts around the base of the plant at the beginning of the growing season and water it in.

Pruning Roses

Detailed information about this special subject can be found in my book "PRUNING". Here are a few easy-to-remember tips.

■ The best-known rule about pruning roses is "always cut back to an outward facing bud." This means exactly what it says. At the juncture of a cane and a leaf formed of five leaflets is a node which will eventually develop into a rose. Find one which faces outward (for good growth and the beauty of the bush) and cut just above it. This rule applies whether you are pruning away dead blooms, cutting flowers at their peak, or pruning right down.

■ Always use a very sharp knife or pruning shears, and cut at a 45′ angle so that the water will run off the cane and not attract bugs.

■ Take as little stem as possible when you are cutting blooms from recently planted bushes. This will allow the leaves which are left to work at full capacity for the bush's growth.

■ The best time to cut blooms for arrangements is in the afternoon.

■ Never prune in fall. Just remove dead foliage and mound earth around the plant (preferably from some other part of the garden). Cover with branches or other mulch, except straw which encourages mice, and wait until spring.

■ In the spring, cut out any canes which are growing inward or rubbing against others, and any obviously dead or broken ones. Leave four strong evenly-spaced canes. Then cut down to the 3rd or 4th outward facing bud on each cane.

■ The way to deal with suckers (shoots growing out of the earth . . . not new canes coming from the bud union) is to yank them out. Cutting them off will just encourage them to grow even more.

Chapter Seven

Perennials

Baby's Breath
(Gypsophila)

Condition	Solution
Light	Sun to partial shade.
Soil	Well-draining, alkaline.
Bloom	July and later.

Baby's Breath is the airy white spray which makes the bouquets for the bride so beautiful. Its graceful and delicate qualities make it just as indispensible in the border to soften the shapes of other plants and add interest. The most durable variety for this purpose is called G. paniculata. Long stems branch out at the top carrying many small flowers — usually white but sometimes pink. Gysophila makes an excellent cut flower for indoor arrangements and lasts a long time.

This plant loves alkaline soil which makes it a good companion for carnations and pinks, as well as delphinium. Add a small spadeful of ground limestone to the planting hole and mix into the planting earth. The soil should also be well-draining so compost or leaf mold should be mixed in along with the lime. Don't add peat moss, though, as it would counter the effects of the lime. You can sow seeds right into the ground or buy plants from the nursery. These plants may have been grafted and its a good idea to plant the

Baby's Breath

bud union just beneath the soil line.

In the spring, work a little limestone into the earth around the plants, and when they start to grow, put tomato cages over them. These will be totally hidden by the grown gypsophilia but keep the floppy ones supported. The main blooming period is in July. You can sheer back after this for renewed growth in late summer. In the fall, cut back and after the ground freezes, mulch with leaves.

Bleeding Heart
(Dicentra)

Condition	Solution
Light	Partial shade.
Soil	Well-cultivated.
Bloom	June to September.

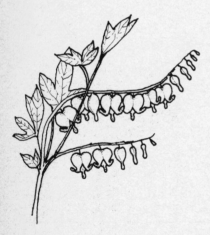

Bleeding Heart

Bleeding Heart is one of the plants which reminds us of the old-fashioned garden. It got its name because the flowers hang from drooping branches and are shaped like little hearts. The most popular colours are red or pink. The foliage is pretty too, and looks like a bush — the airy leaves are attractive all season. Two popular varieties are D. spectabalis and D. Formosa. The first grows up to 3 feet and blooms in May and June very gracefully. The variety D. formosa or Western Bleeding Heart is lower-growing but it blooms all summer.

Choose a spot in the garden where the plants will have room to spread several feet, and in partial to full shade. The soil should be rich and moist so cultivate it first with a lot of organic material like compost or

68

leaf mold. Initially, buy your plants from the nursery. If you want more, divide grown plants in early spring and replant. Most varieties of Bleeding Heart self-snow as well. The new foliage will start to grow at the side of the plant, and if you want it to remain for the following season, be careful not to damage it in fall clean-ups.

Water frequently but don't let the earth get soggy. Pinch out spent blooms and cut back the plant after all the blooms have faded. This is an elegant and graceful addition to the garden and can be used to good advantage in awkward shady areas.

Carnation

(Dianthus)

Condition	Solution
Light	Full sun.
Soil	Alkaline, well-draining.
Bloom	June or longer.

The carnation that we know from the florist shop, with its long stem and large fragrant flower, is a perennial with appeal. However, it is also a complicated flower to take care of which is why it is usually left to the ministrations of professional growers. Very similar but much more cooperative in the border is a variety called D. plumarius — Cottage or Grass Pinks. Sometimes all these names can get confusing. Dianthus is the family to which the carnation belongs. The common name for dianthus is "pinks" because their feathery petals look as if they had been cut with

Carnation

pinking sheers. The Cottage Pinks are lower-growing than the carnation, with matted foliage reaching 6″ in height and the colourful and fragrant flowers rising another 6″ above it. The usual colours are pink, salmon, red, and white, and the foliage is grey-green and fringed like ragged grass.

Buy plants from the nursery and set out in alkaline soil. A handful of limestone added to the planting hole and thoroughly mixed in will usually be enough to bring the pH level up. Plant about 12″ apart in full sun, or morning sun if the summers are really hot. Water when dry. Sheer back after first growth (for renewed bloom) and before winter. These are hardy and long-lived perennials. Mix a little limestone into the earth every spring, and divide every 3 or 4 years in the early spring.

Chrysanthemums
(Chrysanthemums)

Condition	Solution
Light	Full sun to partial shade.
Soil	Average well-draining.
Bloom	Late summer and autumn.

Chrysanthemums are one of the most reliable staples of the perennial garden. There are literally thousands of hybrids and varieties, which makes this flower popular with both the most advanced horticulturalist and the beginning gardener. The flowers are generally from 2″ to 4″ across and are carried on many-branched stems. Chrysanthemums come in all colours except blue, but are most closely identified with sunny and autumnal colours like bronze, yellow and deep red.

Buy in pots at the nursery, and plant in the spring or summer. If you have large plants in pots in the house, you can set these out too. The plants do well in full sun or partial shade, but the afternoon sun shining on them in the autumn and bringing out their colours is something to consider when choosing a location.

Feed every month during the growing season and water regularly. However, don't water at all after the blooms appear. A good way to get bushier plants is to pinch off the top inch of growth on the growing tips from spring until the middle of summer. One of the distinctive things about chrysanthemums is that their roots grow very close to the surface of the earth. This means that you can literally dig the plants up and change their place in the garden with very little damage. It also means that you have to be careful when you are cultivating around the plants with a fork or cultivator. Don't go down too deep or you might damage the roots. Mulch in the summer to prevent weeds. After bloom, cut the plants down to the ground and mulch again after the ground freezes.

Chrysanthemums

Chinese Lantern
(Physalis)

Condition	Solution
Light	Sun or light shade.
Soil	Average.
Bloom	October.

The Chinese lantern makes a colourful dried flower for winter arrangements as well as adding interest to the garden. It grows about 2 feet high on woody stalks, and is distinctive for its brilliant orange calyx which really do look like the red lanterns carried by the Chinese. They can be dried easily. Pick them at their peak, remove the leaves and hang upside down in a dark place with good air circulation. The furnace room is good as long as it's not too hot.

These plants are terribly easy

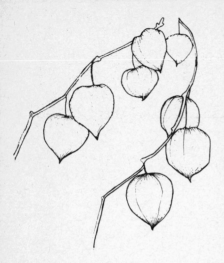

Chinese Lantern

to plant and take care of, and can be used in problem areas of the garden as well as the border. Since they like ordinary soil, you don't have to add any organic amendments. You plant by sowing seeds directly into raked earth in the spring, or by planting cuttings from someone else's garden. Chinese lanterns spread by means of rhizomes, and you don't even have to dig them up to divide. Simply slide your spade down into the earth and lift out the cut-off part. You can control the spread by this method, or get bits for replanting.

The best varieties are P. alkekengi or P. franchetii, and either one provides an easy-to-grow and colourful plant.

Columbine

(Aquilegia)

Condition	Solution
Light	Light shade
Soil	Rich, well-draining.
Bloom	Late spring.

Columbine is a lovely plant with graceful stems holding funnel-shaped flowers. A member of the buttercup family, this flower has many varieties and colours — white, blue, pink, yellow and many bi-colours. "Spring Song" is a variety with mixed colours and many petals. There are dwarf varieties excellent for rock gardens, but generally Columbine grows up to 2 feet. Although the flowers are lovely, they are also short-lived, but the foliage stands out all season for its light silver-green colour and delicate appearance.

You can buy plants at the nursery or sow seeds which will start to grow the following year. Set out in full sun or light shade about 1' apart in soil with a sufficient amount of organic material mixed in. Good drainage is essential. Don't plant in law areas. Mulch to keep the roots cool and maintain a steady degree of moisture, and water fairly often with a double-diluted fertilizer like 5-15-5. Since Columbine is short-lived, sow new seeds every year or plant young seedlings from the nursery.

Remove spent blooms to prevent seed pods from forming and watch out for the signs of leaf miners. If you see their winding trails on leaves growing pale, remove those leaves and spray the plant with Diazinon or malathion.

Columbine

Delphinium
(Delphinium)

Condition	Solution
Light	Morning sun, or full sun.
Soil	Alkaline well-draining.
Bloom	Summer.

Delphinium

There are also bi-coloured flowers available in the D. elatum hybrids in purple, pink and white.

Buy plants from the nursery and set out in soil which has been well-cultivated with compost. Just before setting the plants out, add a small spadeful of lime to the planting holes as these flowers love alkaline soil. Choose a place in full sun, or morning sun if your summers get very hot. Make sure the air circulation will be sufficient but don't put out in a windy spot. Delphinium can grow from 4' to 8' and can get knocked down in strong winds. They are also short-lived, so if you want a steady supply in your border, you'd better set out new plants every couple of years, 2 to 3 feet apart.

Feed in the spring and every month during the growing season with a slow-release fertilizer like 5-15-5 or 5-10-10. Water from underneath to keep the soil moist but don't let it get soggy. A good 2 inches of mulch will keep the soil's moisture level constant. As the spikes

The delphinium is not the easiest perennial to grow, but it is so attractive that most people want to have it in their gardens. The plant has tall spikes of closely packed flowers rising from foliage, at the bottom, and is famous for its beautiful blue.

begin to get tall, tie them to bamboo stakes to keep them upright. Good air circulation should keep them free of mildew, and the mulch will help prevent black spot, but if you see any diseased leaves remove and discard. Then dust the rest with Funginex every couple of weeks.

Foxgloves
(Digitalis purpurea)

Condition	Solution
Light	Light to full shade.
Soil	Moist, well-cultivated.
Bloom	June to August.

There are a number of explanations about this plant's name, but perhaps it is best to settle for the most fanciful one — that the little flowers would make nice gloves for little foxes. For many years, foxgloves were used to treat heart disease in folk medicine and the drug digitalis is still used today. The flowers themselves are long spikes with small bell-shaped blooms up and down them. Common fox-gloves, D. purpurea, come in many colours including pink, purple, white and red. They have leafy stems and dense foliage at the bottom, with some varieties reaching 4 feet. D. grandiflora is closely related to the common floxglove but blooms a bit later — in July and August — and has densely

Foxgloves

packed blooms in a light creamy yellow. It does best in the shade.

Choose a spot in the garden which is in partial shade and where the ground won't get dried out by the sun in the summer. Cultivate it well with peat moss and set out nursery stock about 1 to 2 feet apart in the spring. Although foxgloves are really a biennial, they self-seed, so once you've got them planted, they tend to stay around longer than two years.

However, it's a good idea to set out new plants on a regular basis to give a constant growth.

Care is easy. Mulch to keep roots cool and water occasionally. Stake the plants at the bottom with bamboo stakes to keep them upright. Let old blooms stay on the plants if you want them to set out seeds for the following year, and spray the plants every couple of weeks with Funginex to prevent mildew and black spot disease.

Hosta or Plantain Lily

(Hosta)

Condition	Solution
Light	Partial shade.
Soil	Rich, well-cultivated.
Bloom	June to October.

This beautiful plant is a real winner in the perennial garden. It is famous for its wonderful leaves which are grey, bright green or varigated. Each leaf can grow 1 foot high with the wide-forming plants which are 4 feet across. A variety called the Blue-Leaf Plantain (H. sieboldiana) has green leaves which turn powdery blue. In July, small and fragrant flowers start to bloom. They are usually white and look like little lilies.

This plant has many varieties and colours. Catalogues will be able to show you part of this amazing assortment.

Get plants from the nursery and set out in soil which has leaf mold or other composted material mixed in. Choose a spot in partial shade or filtered light, and keep the soil mulched for cool roots. Water enough to keep the earth moist. Plantain Lily is not only good at the back of the border — it is also excellent around the patio or pool as long as it isn't in direct sun all the time.

Groom faded blooms and stems during growing season. In the spring, work some manure into the soil around the plants with a gardening fork. In the fall, mulch the earth as soon as the ground freezes. With a little care, hosta will live for up to 25 years and be one of your best investments.

Hosta or Plantain Lily

Iris, Bearded-species
and hybrids

Condition	Solution
Light	Full sun.
Soil	Slightly acid, well-draining.
Bloom	May and June.

Also known as the flag iris, this is one of the most popular perennials. There are so many hybrids and varieties that whole books have been written about them, international clubs formed, and professionals compete with them. Still, the amateur gardener can also get a lot of pleasure from a stand of iris without getting bogged down in masses of information. Usually, your nursery will have the type which has proven to be the best in your area. The plant gets its name because it has a "beard". The three outer petals on the flower are called "falls" because they fall away from the three inner petals. These are called "standards" because they stand erect. In between these sets of petals is a fuzzy bit called the "beard".

Iris, Bearded —

species and hybrids

Plant nursery stock in earth well-cultivated with organic material other than peat moss. Choose a spot in full sun. If you are using rhizomes place them in the earth so that the leaves will grow outward about 1 foot apart.

Water from underneath but don't sog up the earth, and feed once in the spring with 5-15-5 and again after the blooms have faded. Watch out for iris borers as they can eventually kill the plants. They leave a trail of slime on the leaves. Remove any infected leaves and try to dig out the borer. Spray with Sevin every couple of weeks in the spring and always remove foliage in the fall to discourage the borers. Divide clumps every 4 years and replant. One fan of leaves is a good size to replant.

Lily Of The Valley

(Convallaria)

Condition	Solution
Light	Shade.
Soil	Moist, richly composted.
Bloom	May and early June.

Lily of the valley is a spring ground cover with very fragrant white flowers shaped like small bells which are held on long stalks. They are famous not only for their delicate appearance and scent, but the musical round which children still sing. "White coral bells upon a slender stalk, Lily of the valley deck our garden walk." The flowers, along with their masses of large glossy leaves, can deck your walk, or your deck, or any troublesome corner of the garden as long as it's in the shade. The only variety grown here is C. majalis which reaches a height of about 8 inches.

Lily Of The Valley

Choose a shady area with soil which may have been naturally composted already ... beside fir hedges for example. Add a good deal of other compost and mix in. Buy bedding plants or "eyes" at the nursery and set out 8 inches apart. When the tops die down in the summer, work some manure into the soil around the plants with a garden fork or hand cultivator. The plants will spread by themselves, but if they get out of control, simply cut down through the earth with your spade and remove the unwanted parts.

Lily of the valley are easy to grow and can be a pleasant way to start the summer. They are also good picked and used in sprays ... although they have a tendency to go brown after a time ... and the smell is justly famous.

Lupin
(Lupinus)

Condition	Solution
Light	Sun.
Soil	Slightly acid, well-draining.
Bloom	June.

Lupin

Lupins are lovely but since they do best in areas with cool moist summers, people living in hot summer areas might be a bit disappointed if the plants stall and refuse to grow. A cool area in the garden which still gets some sun is ideal, and lupins are certainly worth trying. Tall spikes are covered with pea-like flowers in vibrant colours including red, purple and salmon. They bloom around June, but afterwards don't remove the foliage — just the stalks. The greenery will add beauty to the border and strength to the plants.

Buy your peat pots from the nursery and set out in groups of 3 to 5 in soil well-mixed with damp peat moss. Russell Hybrids are the lupins most successfully cultivated. They grow up to 3 feet and should be planted about 18 inches apart. The dwarf variety is half that height and spread.

Mulch to keep the roots cool and water just enough to keep the soil damp but not wet. Feed occasionally with a fertilizer low in nitrogen like 5-15-5, and dust with Funginex to keep down mildew and rust. If you are successful with your lupins, they will spread. Divide in the fall of the second season and replant.

Peony
(Paenonia)

Condition	Solution
Light	Full sun to partial shade.
Soil	Slightly acid, well-draining.
Bloom	Early summer.

Peonies take up a fair bit of room in the border but they are worth it for the beautiful flowers they produce. The plants have thick stands of large lush leaves with large flowers rising out of them. The blooms have a delightful fragrance. Different varieties will have different petal formations but the doubles with their frilly edges are the most spectacular, and white, pink and red are the standard colours. The most popular and easily grown variety for the border is the herbaceous peony (P. lactiflora). The flowers are wonderful for cutting, but be sure to shake any ants off before you bring them into the house.

A stand can grow 4 feet high and 4 feet wide so choose a spot with some space around it, in the sun. Peonies like an acid soil so cultivate with plenty of damp peat moss before planting. Buy plants at the nursery and set out in fairly deep holes, or get "eyes" (named for the little buds at the top of the roots) and plant 3 to 5 at once about 1 inch deep.

Peonies are long-lived and

Peony

can take over the border if you let them. Always cut right down to the ground before winter, and every other fall, dig up and divide into clumps of 5 "eyes" for replanting. Water occasionally during growing season but make sure water drains away quickly. Add some apple cider vinegar to the water every once in a while to give the plants some natural acid.

Phlox

(Phlox paniculata, Phlox subulata)

Condition	Solution
Light	Full sun.
Soil	Rich and well-draining.
Bloom	Spring and summer.

Phlox

pletely covered with cicles of flowers about 1 inch across growing 2 to 3 feet high. Long dark-green leaves surround the spikes.

Buy plants from the nursery and set out in soil well-mixed with organic materials, about 16 inches apart. Get varieties of P. paniculata for flowers which blooms in the summer and then off and on until the fall. P. sublata is low-growing and dense. It blooms in early spring and makes a good ground cover.

Water in the middle of the summer if the weather gets hot. Remove spent blooms as soon as you can to prevent seed pods from forming as this will halt further flowering. Divide in the spring and replant. You should spray with Funginex every cou;e of weeks during the growing season to prevent rust and powdery mildew.

Phlox has bell-shaped flowers on tall spikes in a range of pure colours — reds and pinks, purples and lavender, and white. The heads of the spikes are com-

Poppy, Oriental

(Papover)

Condition	Solution
Light	Full sun.
Soil	Average but well-draining.
Bloom	Early summer.

Poppies have single-petalled flowers supported on long stems. The flowers are quite large — from 4" to 10" across — and are dramatic and showy. The foliage is at the bottom. Red, the most popular and stunning colour, is usually set off with a black centre. Poppies come in other colours, though. Bi-coloured varieties in white and purple, pink and red, and white and pink are effective. There was a superstition at one time that poppies would make you go to sleep because some varieties are the source of opium. This belief was further advanced, for children at least, when Dorothy and her friends were seen falling asleep running through a field of poppies on their way to Oz. The gardener will find, however, that this flower's vibrant colours will be more likely to wake people up than send them into slumber.

Poppy, Oriental

Poppies like average soil as long as it drains well and is located in the sun. You can even use them for a bit of show in an awkward part of the garden as long as it's on a slight rise. Buy plants from the nursery and set out in the early spring about 15 inches apart. The flowers grow up to 3 feet high and will need support. Divide every 5 years in the late summer. If you want to cut the blooms and bring them into the house, plunge them immediately into water *after* burning the ends with the flame of a match or lighter.

Primrose
(Primula)

Condition	Solution
Light	Morning sun.
Soil	Rich, moist, well-draining.
Bloom	Early spring.

Primrose

The English primrose, or Primula vulgaris, is one of the most colourful and welcome harbingers of spring. Lovely clusters of flowers can grow up to 2 feet high, and although primroses are available in a wide assortment of colours, yellow is still the favourite with many people. There are a number of varieties with P. polyanthus being the best known. This has all colours except blue and red.

The primrose likes soil which is cool and moist. Add lots of compost to earth in an area which gets morning sun or partial shade. It also likes soil slightly on the acid side so add peat moss to bring the pH down. Set bedding plants out about 12 inches apart and plant along with other spring blooming perennials like violets.

During its blooming period, the primrose develops many blooms which are good for cutting. Picking the flowers will also help to encourage new growth. Every couple of years, you should dig the plants up and divide the roots for replanting. Apart from that, its an easy-care and long-living plant which gladdens the weary heart spring after spring.

Ranunculus
(Ranunculus aconitifolius)

Condition	Solution
Light	Sun or partial shade.
Soil	Rich and moist.
Bloom	April to June.

These flowers are relatives of the buttercup and some varieties, with their butter-yellow flowers, illustrate that relationship. A variety called "Florepleno" has double-flowered white flowers like pincushions. Both colours seem to catch the sun and shine — adding glisten to the early perennial garden. Ranunculus grows in clumps on slender stems with foliage along the stalks, and blooms in April. Floreplene blooms in May and June. The clumps grow from 1 to 2 feet with a similar spread.

All ranunculus love moist rich earth so be sure to add lots of peat moss, leaf mold or manure to the soil before planting. Choose a spot in sun or light shade — although the flowers look so fine in the sun that this is probably the best choice. Set out nursery plants about 18 inches apart and keep the soil moist but never soggy.

These flowers are easy to care for. When they come into bloom, pinch off any dead flowers right away. This will encourage strong new growth.

Keep the soil underneath the plants well-mulched. Every couple of years, divide the plants for better blooms. Plant alone for a dramatic effect, or with more colourful plants as contrast.

Ranunculus

Red-Hot Poker
(Kniphofia uvaria)

Condition	Solution
Light	Full sun.
Soil	Composted and well-draining.
Bloom	August and September.

The brilliant velvety spikes on this flower give it its descriptive name. Grassy foliage mounds up to 3 feet and is 2 to 3 feet across. The spikes or "pokers" grow up to 4 feet and can stand erect or gently droop. Many varieties have different colours like white, creams and yellows, but the most outstanding are the flaming reds and oranges.

Red-Hot Poker

Buy plants from the nursery and plant in soil which has been well-cultivated with organic material. It's a good idea to add home-made compost which will continue to break down into humus over the years as this is a long-living plant. Leaf mold is excellent. Although the plants are large, they will be fully grown in 4 years and will last for years after that. Make sure you plant them where they will get as much sun as possible and leave room for them to spread. Ask for varieties which bloom at the beginning and middle of the growing season as well, so you can have continuous colour.

Gently fork manure into the earth around the plants every spring and water occasionally in hot spells. In the fall, cut down and mulch over winter as soon as the ground freezes to prevent heaving.

Sedum or Stonecrop
(Sedum)

Condition	Solution
Light	Sun to light shade.
Soil	Average to sandy.
Bloom	August to frost.

Sedum is more commonly called stonecrop because of the ability of some species to grow on stony ledges. The most popular of the 350 species is S. spectabile with a variety called "Brilliant" which has raspberry red flowers. It attracts butterflies and sometimes humming-birds as well. The plants have a good-looking foliage — fleshy, slightly waxy and grey-green — and large heads made up of small colourful flowers. Best colours are shades of red, but there are also pinks and whites. Another hybrid is called "Autumn Joy". It grows to about the same height — 1 to 2 feet — but its deep-pink flowers gradually turn to bronze as the autumn comes.

Sedum doesn't like too much moisture so a light soil is good. You can mix it with peat moss for even better blooms and to help drainage. Buy plants at the nursery and set out about 18 inches apart in a sunny spot or one which gets filtered light.

This is truly an easy-care plant. It hardly ever needs water or fertilizer, and there doesn't seem to be very much that makes it sick. It is long-lived and all you have to do is divide it in the spring every couple of years to encourage blooming.

Sedum or Stonecrop

Shasta Daisy
(Chrysanthemum)

Condition	Solution
Light	Full sun or partial shade.
Soil	Average to well-cultivated.
Bloom	Early summer to frost.

The daisy may seem a good deal humbler than some its more exotic perennial partners, but who can resist its pretty face and sterling qualities. The flowers are white with yellow eyes and many flared petals, and measure 2 to 3 inches across. They are carried on long wiry stems and make excellent cut flowers. They bloom continuously from early summer until the frost.

Set out plants from the nursery in the spring. Choose a spot in full sun, although daisies will also do well in partial shade. Cultivate the earth with damp peat moss or other organic material. Leave 1 to 2 feet between new plants.

Keep flowers picked to encourage new blooms and water occasionally — but don't let the soil get too wet. Feed once a month with a fertilizer like 5-15-5 until the middle of the summer. Divide in the spring and replant. Although these plants can grow up to 3 or 4 feet high, they make good middle of the border flowers because of their continuous bloom. The daisy is a good flower for the beginning gardener due to its easy care and hardy nature.

Shasta Daisy

Tiger Lily
(L. tigrinum)

Condition	Solution
Light	Full sun to partial shade.
Soil	Moist, well-cultivated.
Bloom	August.

There are literally thousands of varieties of lily, and they just keep coming. Anyone interested in more detailed literature can read one of the many books on the subject. For the backyard gardener, however, some simple information about these popular plants can be helpful.

One of the most familiar and easiest to care for is the Tiger Lily — called L. tigrinum. These bright-orange flowers with black or brown spots are narrow-throated and trumpet-shaped. When they die down, the sword-like leaves of the plant are also attractive. The flowers have a pleasant aroma and can grow up to 5 feet high.

Get plants at the nursery and set out in early spring. Cultivate the soil well before planting with compost or peat moss, and leave about 2 to 3 feet between plants to allow for spread. The plants will thrive equally well in full sun or partial shade.

Water occasionally in the spring to strengthen the blooms but don't add fertilizer as this will encourage too much foliage. Mulch well around the roots to keep the soil consistently moist, and in the winter after the soil freezes. Divide every 5 years. This plant is colourful, reliable and easy to care for — even if it is only one of thousands.

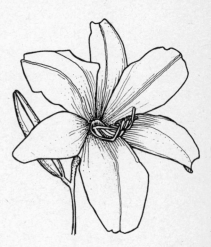

Tiger Lily

Violet
(Viola)

Condition	Solution
Light	Sun to partial shade.
Soil	Ordinary to well composted.
Bloom	April to July.

There are over 300 species of violets, one of which is V. odo-rata or the purple violets which bloom in the spring. It used to be popular for ladies to pin

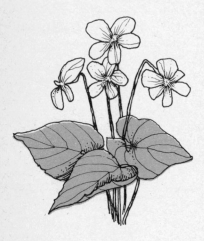

Violet

bunches of these sweet-smelling flowers to their coats, and violets still have trails of romance wafting after them. In the garden, they are low-growing, and each plant spreads about 1 foot. They can be planted as a ground cover, in a spring garden or in awkward spots at the bottom of the yard. You might also consider a hardy stain called V. carnuta. This is a relative but much more noticea-ble. It grows as high as a foot, has a good spread, and blooms from May to July.

Violets will grow in ordinary soil but do better in soil with some wet compost added. Buy plants from the nursery at first and set out 1 foot apart. Every spring, work some composted manure into the soil with a garden fork or hand cultivator, and after the plants are estab-lished, divide in the fall and replant. Keep both varieties picked, or pinch out blooms as soon as they fade. This will keep the blooming period going longer.

Notes

Notes

Notes

Notes

Notes

Cullen Garden Guides

A series of 8 garden guides written especially for Canadian garden conditions. Written by Mark Cullen, one of Canada's leading gardening experts, these handy guides are easy to read, yet packed full of the information you need for every situation. Titles in the series include:

HOUSEPLANTS by Mark Cullen $5.95

LAWNS AND LANDSCAPING by Mark Cullen $5.95

WEEDS, PESTS AND DISEASES by Mark Cullen $5.95

ANNUALS by Mark Cullen $5.95

PERENNIALS AND ROSES by Mark Cullen $5.95

PRUNING by Mark Cullen $5.95

CONTAINER GARDENING by Mark Cullen $5.95

If you can't find your favourite Cullen Garden Guide where you shop, you can obtain a copy by sending **$5.95** plus **50¢** postage for each book to:

Summerhill Press Ltd.
5 Clarence Square
Toronto, Ontario M5V 1H1

Please allow three weeks for delivery